The Selected
Poems of
Clive Branson

The Selected
Poems of
Clive Branson
edited by
Richard Knott

Smokestack Books
1 Lake Terrace,
Grewelthorpe, Ripon
HG4 3BU
info@smokestack-books.co.uk
www.smokestack-books.co.uk

ISBN 978-1-7391730-0-5

Smokestack Books
is represented
by Inpress Ltd

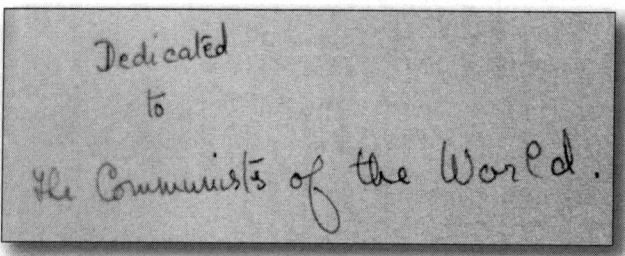

Clive Branson's handwritten dedication to his first
privately printed collection.

Contents

Clive Branson, Artist and Poet

The artist and poet Clive Branson was born in Ahmednagar, India, in 1907, the son of a major in the regular Indian army. Privately educated at Bedford School, the expectation was that Clive would go on to work for the Hong Kong and Shanghai Bank. In the event, his growing social conscience, combined with a passionate desire to paint, saw him go on to study at the Slade School of Art in London. The teaching at the Slade, however, disappointed him to the extent that he walked out, intending to find his own way as an artist.

Already left-leaning as a young man, Clive Branson would become a convinced and committed Communist by the 1930s. His political views were greatly influenced by what he saw of London's poverty, the evident inequalities in the capital and its widespread poor housing. He was also excited by events in post-revolutionary Russia. Clive and his wife Noreen briefly joined the Independent Labour Party in the autumn of 1931, but he soon left to concentrate his energies on the local community in Battersea where the couple lived. There he began a weekly street paper, *Revolt,* selling it from door to door. Later both Bransons joined the Communist Party and Clive decided to abandon his career as an artist, choosing instead to become a political activist, selling the *Daily Worker* at Clapham Junction, canvassing, selling literature and speaking at factory gates. Noreen Branson, meanwhile, worked for Harry Pollitt, the secretary of the Communist Party of Great Britain.

When the Spanish Civil War began in 1936, Clive was keen to volunteer and fight for the Spanish Republic, only for Harry Pollitt to persuade him that the Party in England had greater need of his talents. 'Put it off for now,' Pollitt said, with a smile and Clive's request to head for Spain early in 1937 was firmly refused. Instead Branson was put in charge of guiding volunteers from all over the United Kingdom through the capital and onwards to the Spanish war, the would-be fighters leaving by the 'Red Train' from Victoria Station.

It was 1938 before the Party leadership agreed that Branson should be free to volunteer. He left for Spain at the beginning of January that year, evading the attentions of Special Branch by only a matter of days. He underwent training at a camp in Albacete over a five-week period before going to the front, in charge of a group of twenty men, all of them poorly equipped and many without rifles. In March he was captured during the battle of Calaceite, paraded in front of the world's press in Saragossa and then taken to the prison at San Pedro de Cardeña where he was incarcerated for three months. Nine miles from Burgos, it was a forbidding monastery: overcrowded, gloomy, primitive, rat-infested and cold.

In this grim captivity, Branson's salvation was his poetry. He wrote about the durability and courage of his fellow prisoners; the weather, the 'grip of prison', the loss of freedom, the enforced idleness ('men die/while we sit and in the hot sun lie'), and the enemy ('this Fascist's bloody name'). In the summer of 1938 Branson was moved to a prison camp in Palencia, 55 miles south-west of Burgos. The Italian-run regime was less brutal than San Pedro and here Branson could write and was encouraged to draw, producing among other things more than fifty portraits of his fellow prisoners. At one point he was commissioned by the camp commandant to paint a set of pictures of the camp.

Branson was eventually released from captivity in the autumn of 1938. He returned to England, his political certainties as strong as ever. As war threatened, he began painting again, landscapes of rural England. Such peace would be short-lived and once again Branson found himself in uniform, this time with the Royal Armoured Corps: 'C' Squadron, 54th Training Regiment, based at Perham Down camp, close to Salisbury Plain. He found life in the British Army dispiriting and tedious, while the wider political context was equally unpromising. He felt, for example, out of kilter with Britain's war strategy, believing that 'Britain will fight to the last Russian.'

Eventually, early in 1942, Branson decided to explore the possibility of becoming an official war artist but the initial response was unpromising and soon after he was posted to India in May 1942. He arrived in Bombay (as it then was) and was profoundly shocked by the city's poverty. However, India's people and land-scape were such that he felt encouraged to sketch again and contemplate life as a painter once the war was finally over: 'What a people this is for painting!' By 31 May 1942, Branson was stationed at Gulunche Camp, near Poona (Pune).

His time in India – some nineteen months or so – was, for the most part, spent waiting for battle to begin. He taught himself Hindustani; dreamed of life after the war was over; fulminated in letters home about Churchill's refusal to open a second front against the Germans; visited his birthplace, Ahmednagar, in June 1943; and worried whether he would 'command my tank as a Communist ought.'

Inevitably the routine of life in camp had to end, replaced by his unit being uncomfortably established close to the Japanese positions, in primitive, uncertain conditions. It was, as he wrote to Noreen, 'nearing zero hour.' Instead of painting or poetry, there were the mundane preparations for combat: getting kit clean and ready, and 'darning, buttons, vests, socks and pants.'

Then, in January 1944, events began to move uncomfortably fast: Branson was promoted to Troop Sergeant and, on the night of 24 January, his unit moved into action. By the following morning he and his men were caught up in a full-scale battle. Clive's letter home on 4 February included a sonnet with an ominous last line: 'When life has gone, then where does death begin?'

From that point, his letters dried up while the all-consuming Battle of the Admin Box developed. On 25 February, with the battle won, British tanks were ordered to make an assault on Point 315. Soon after, the tank that Branson commanded was hit by enemy fire. Troop Sergeant Clive Branson, who had been standing with his head out of the turret, was killed. He was just 36 years old.

In the same year that Branson died, the Communist Party published a book of his letters, *British Soldier in India* with an introduction by Harry Pollitt. It was a book that the playwright Sean O'Casey described as 'the best book that the Communist Party has given us' and among other things included some examples of Clive's poetry. As far back as 1932 he had produced a privately published collection of his poetry and, after his death, his work appeared in various collections, for example, *The Penguin Book of Spanish Civil War Verse*.

This volume of poetry is the first opportunity to read the full range of Branson's work: verse prompted by his political commitment, his experience as a prisoner of war, his empathy with the poor and downtrodden in both India and England, and his love of landscape, the natural world, his art and his family.

Clive Branson is better remembered as an artist than as a poet. Five of his paintings are held by the Tate Gallery in London: a portrait of a worker painted in the 1930s, a still life from 1940 and three more typical pieces depicting the selling of the *Daily Worker* outside a factory; aeroplanes over London and a city scene overshadowed by a barrage balloon. But he was a fine poet too and he treasured both arts, writing poetry even near the end, close to the Japanese lines, as well as sketching and planning what he would be free to paint once the war ended.

Branson's early verse is less overtly political than his later work. In those early days he wrote about landscape, both urban and rural: about sunrise, tulips, the Thames, the London underground. Even so, the dedication in his first collection emphatically nails his red colours to the mast: the book is for 'The Communists of the World.' As the world drifted towards war, through the Thirties, Branson's poetry acquired a much more committed and passionate political stance.

This collection begins, not with his early work, but with 'The International', a poem which encapsulates what sets his verse apart. Here he displays the poetic virtues of immediacy and clarity, as well as his strong belief in the power of the people: *'One man, one woman, humanity/ The 'International' our theme.'* The Spanish Civil War, imprisonment in a fascist prison, his enlistment in the British Army, the cultural shock of India and its poverty, the looming engagement with the Japanese army in Burma – all shaped him and his poetry. When he died, aged 36, he was as committed politically as he ever was, his verse just as impassioned.

In 1980, Penguin published its *Book of Spanish Civil War Verse*. The poets included the familiar and much lauded: Auden,

Stephen Spender, Louis MacNeice, C Day Lewis and Laurie Lee. Clive Branson is well represented in the anthology, along with a number of other lesser-known poets, including John Cornford, Tom Wintringham and Sylvia Townsend Warner. Branson's work does not suffer by way of comparison. It is noticeable too that, arguably, he alone of the poets never lost his belief in the communist view of the world, his certainty. That derived from his work and experiences in pre-war London, Spain and India. His work Sean O'Casey described as displaying 'a sensitive touch, deep, delightful and lasting.' That sensitivity is evident in his poems too.

Soon after the Penguin anthology came out, Noreen Branson wrote to the editor, Valentine Cunningham, saying that she and her daughter 'were happy to see (the poems) in print after all these years.' She took issue with parts of his 'Introduction' however, regretting his 'distortion of the motives' of some people and his failure to point out that the Soviet Union had armed the Spanish Republic when no other country would. Clive would have wholeheartedly approved.

Richard Knott
2023

Spain's
Civil War

The International

We'd left our training base
And by the time night fell
Stood facing the Universe
Singing *The International.*

I remember it so well
Waiting in the station yard
The darkness stood around still
And the stars, masses, stared.

That's when I first understood
One is never alone in this fight.
I'd thought the 'goodbye' was for good
And left *all* behind that night.

But everything new that I meet,
No matter how strange and uncertain,
Holds something familiar that
Proves the fight is still on.

How often I've marched, and marching
I sang of an England unseen,
Watched the great crowds gathering
And the tramp of their feet beat in tune.

Even in the grip of prison
I joined in the singing of millions
As they wait at their wayside station
That leads to the battle lines.

I'm singing in every country
Where I tread through the streets of Time
One man, one woman, humanity
The International our theme.

January 1940

December 1936, Spain

You! English working men!
Can't you hear the barrage creeping
that levels the Pyrenees?

Is time intangible
that bears so audible
and visible a thing?

Can't you hear the children and women cry
where the Fascist bomb
makes the people's home
a tomb for you and me?

Can't you see the gashes in the street
where our people stumble
when the city trembles?
Can't you smell the rose held in the teeth
tighter than death?

They who lie so still
with no Cross,
only this, their courage, their faith
manures the barren earth
for new trees
to spring up the hill-side to the very sky.

That we should be insensible at such a time
Makes deafness kill and peace the bloodier crime.

June 1939

On Being Questioned After Capture: Alcañiz

I stood before my questioner who asked
'Why leave home?
Why have you come?
Why?' He must have guessed
'Because he is a Communist.'

I thought of all the answers I could give
whether death is correct or whether to save
life for a rainy day
and told a lie to cheat his bullet with a word
to use a bullet afterward

On him the bigger lie – a conscript
'volunteer' to rape Spain where she slept
to save his own skin
he had come when he sought 'The Leader' on his hands and
knees
To crush a thousand years in half an hour
To make Guernica
a wilderness.

I could wait and so could lie
for adjournment to another court
meanwhile to live on my bended knee
to make occasion for another start.
I could imitate the victor, cringe
till I and the world beyond
take our revenge.

1939

Lines Written in a Book of Drawings

done by the order of the Commandant of the Italian Camp

These drawings needed a little freedom,
The eye and hand of man enjoying life.
Great Art demands fulfilment of a dream
Of human peace and friendship, no more strife.

On being ordered to copy a large signature of MUSSOLINI

under a slogan written on the camp wall

For years I've trained, burnt out my sight, not spared
my health, my strength, my life's too tender flame.
I strove to heights no former vision dared –
to scrawl in black this Fascist's bloody name.

Prisoners

Like stones on stones
peeling potatoes
prisoners were
seated in a circle
seeing each other
looking at potatoes
young and old ones.

San Pedro, 1938

The Aeroplane

This winged machine that cancels distance out.
New steel Icarus senseless to the sun.
Would have Da Vinci end what he'd begun
knowing his dream materialised? – the rout
of innocents from field and home – the shout
of joy to spot an aeroplane. Tis done
The metal bird now sings and man has won
Power to touch the stars or turn about.

Small looks the pilot below the wings' spread.
Ailerons quiver. The propeller roars.
This time-derisive bird, perfect to plan,
Takes off. Trees become weed size. Earth withdraws.
It wheels to find his course. Then straight ahead
Springs to achieve the destiny of man.

San Pedro, 1938

The Red Airforce

Continual changes in the layout of time
prove that the stagnant makes from its own womb
breeding a sea of wings, thin as the air
and seemingly as lawless, with no law
other than that implicit in itself.

High on the shoulder of time's recent wave,
part of the deep and nearest to the sun,
gigantic eagles jealous of no one
in formation gather climbing wheel beyond wheel
And the worm, man, sings from his cloud of steel.

The 1930s

Zero Hour

At the crack of dawn when
Babies are waking
Grip the air in their fingers
As the new dawn mingles
In the last shades of night
The distant fringes
Of the earth catch alight.
The little child lingering
On the precincts of sleep
Presses her face in the pillow again.

An extract from the original draft in Clive Branson's notebook.

Light's splendour inflicts itself upon earth.
All the birds whistling, hooters screaming,
Clocks striking, people shouting,
Frighten the new day to hurry up,
To get going.

Latest events litter the pavements
Along with the tickets to yesterday.
The acts of the past have gone to dust
For the refuse cart to take away
To keep the city clean now
To build a city on tomorrow.

Men grope for their rifles, hand grenades.
Tanks out of varied hiding begin to move.
Night bombers fly counter to the sun.
Death occupies the glades where men made love.
Children understand the screams of intrusion.
This morning is no midwife to our birth.

No! Not like the sun do the dead repeat
The farce of their eternal repetition.
The lines of time reach on never to meet.
Light fades out before the end of vision.
Turn on the artificial planets
That swarm about the corners of our streets.
Turn on the headlights and the neon-signs.
The peaks of life aren't gained by blind obedience
To the shortcomings of the sun. Now mountains
Whose high purpose only the eagles know.
In the cities' darkness used to light the streets
So sensitive the switch to the fingers of the night
Before the blackout restored the natural gloom
Continuous with day.

The scream of bombs and winds from wings of death
Kindle the stars among the burnt-out ashes
Of times that no-one remembers, no one cares,
Passed away.

Tasks Before the XIII Party Congress

When water is like corrugated iron
and almost as still.
When the sky is like the inverted lake
and gripped by inert trees, tentacled earth.
This is the archway we walk through for years
leisurely picking up new thoughts like friends
till one would think life had nothing urgent,
was nothing but the gutter of a long street
with the prospect of lining an arterial road,
only the parallel of a railway line
leading the will along its safe known track
to another station, or terminus, or back
again. This part of our journey is hard.
We begin to gauge all motion with similar
underrating accuracy to a few feet
and forget there will be accidents, points to change,
disasters to avoid and organised difficulties
to be overcome with a human locomotive
of which we are but the driver,
the expression of its speed, its possibilities.
Must learn to take it from the shed, leave it never.

December 1934

Paris, 1929

I watched a green leaf falling to the ground
Meanwhile a young man came and went.
I saw the shadow of an elm had moved
And Death incite eternity.
A white cloud slowly passed before the sun
I wondered where the sun had fled;
A sparrow left the thicket near my side;
The sun returned, no more that bird.

I listened to a thrush I could not see,
It was good to hear a voice I could not see
Be chanted to and not yet understand.
Why try to learn the meaning of that song?
Life was a dream – I slept – I heard that song;
When I awake, perhaps I'll understand.

Forward

Because it's time for a revolution.
To end the beating-up of man by man,
To do away with the police nark, stool pigeon, assassin
Judge, gaol.

Because in the common people
We have found something much more beautiful
Than king, God or individual;
That is bad reason
To blunt the nature of our fellow men,
Their will
To climb the steep hill, strip in the sun,
Walk along the river bank, watch the water fowl, to fish
Or sit lazily sucking the juicy end of rich grass,
To take one's girl on a pillion ride
Away from the town down to the sea side.
The writer who says he has no time to care
For the daffodil or cowslip shames
The very revolution he proclaims.
He is no better than the millionaire
Who clears the ground of trees, shrubs, weeds
To make his lawns monotonously green
Forbidden to all except the mowing machine.

Don't insult the bugger on the dole.
He loves the taste and smell of a good meal –
Sure! – but he loves as well
Fresh air, a salty breeze and brown earth still.

It is for these, the joy of being in a man
That the factory hand is ready to risk all,
Can take what's coming to him, and rebel.

Let every Englishman fight for this cause –
Communism is English! Freedom is Ours!

A Song: Lenin to Gorky

We will drink deep of the white wine of Capri
Gorky, you and I, when the day-long finger
Will have cleaned from the earth all tyranny we
Now mean to be ended with rapid anger.

Gone, gone will the time of our fighting be when
The hymn of the wine we'll ring together
With the thunder of clapping and the laughter of men
With whom we worked hard in the day long over.

December 1934

To C Day Lewis

You labour through wastes of depression.
An oasis, a palm tree, a well
you kick for a tombstone. The lesson?
On the beach there's only one pebble,
only one among all.

At the foot of new waves you were jilted.
Think! Shall you think like the sea?
Or would you the white cliffs were lifted
yet higher before they're to be
flat as eternity?

3 July 1935

I Stay
for You

The Sun

The Sun when it begins to climb
Lingers on the crest of time,
Even the sensate butterfly
Flutters ere it die.

The early mist lies on the hills
Until the air with light fills
And so in life I stay for you
Waiting to die too.

Tulips

You strain for the light, for new life,
And lift your supplicating mouths
For pure air,
Your feeble wings lie
Down the vase folded;
And red petals die.

Dwindle into Moors

Dwindle into moors below the aeroplane.
At Zero hour for the human race
After the shout of 'Contact'
Freedom rises curving into space.
Watch the speed. Hear the direction. Wait.
This quintessence of engineering crashes
Into a transparent insect's flight.
Journeys aren't measured by miles between places
Since distance spelt the problem of supply
Where is the victory if the soldier dies?

Smooth movement screens by addition tumult.
Turmoil, pain, doubt, anger, surprises
Stop a revolution; no peace is the result,
No sitting sunning in the park but crises
Yawning factories vomit men and women.
A beautiful bomb rocks our baby's cradle.
How warm for a while the child sleeps.

When the Summer Follows

When the Summer follows, driving
The bees from sleep on honey'd quest
Where multitudes of flowers spring
Intently from earth's ripened breast,
And sprinkles constellations down
On the near-completed gown.

The caterpillar patiently
Spins deftly all its silken shroud
Hiding itself invisibly
In an impenetrable cloud
And slumbers in the tight cocoon
Unnoticed, as the sleeping moon.

For long it stays so deeply still
As motionless when one might hear
The movement of a bird's wings fill
The silence all about a mere;
And the lowly chrysalis hides
From where the heedful time glides.

Patient, as a summer evening
Waits the slow arriving shadow
Thrown from God's eyes brighter seeming
To the benighted earth below,
Hangs through a long-neglected term
The dissembled working worm.

Again an all-unfolding Spring
Ensues in death-like Winter's stead
It feels a subtle fingering
About each shuttled silken thread
It feels a strange instinctive charm
Penetrate its outward calm.

Through a space the quick sensations
Vibrate its still sleepy waking,
And no little emanations
Issue from its gentle changing
No stray beams illumine the darkness
Though the fount of light progress.

To Noreen

I have seen you bear the cup and drink
Sipping the warm minutes of evening
And winnow the grey hairs of day
From pretended darkness, smoking.

You counted the uneatable 'beggarman'
And watched the taxis move up in their rank
Heard the footsteps of the people
Heard the clock register each new blank.

So whiled away an age have you and I
Sitting and listening to the stars
Caring not how many filled the sky
Nor was that music written which has faded.

And will you drink black coffee till the moon
Lights the round bottom of the cup you hold
Or hearing the clouds no more, get bored soon
And leave me on the pavement thirsting?

1931

Noreen Branson

Why Do You Write to Me?

Why do you write to me saying
Your letters are useless and dead
For time is on our love laying
Yearly a sod to fill love's bed?

Your letters are always telling
The tale of our love to these eyes
And a few tears over-welling
Renew the old tale while it dies.

I know that our ill love's dying
In the bed that the world has made,
But we shall be with our love lying
Before the last sods have been laid.

Have They Told You?

Have they told you how my dreams
Of you have always lied
And now that you have gone it seems
That my wild-rose had died?

Have they told you how I keep
A flower at my side,
A new rose that I love as deep
As my wild rose that died?

Have they told you how I chose
Someone to be my bride?
I could not live without a rose
Since my wild-rose had died.

Music

We laid our shadows on the floor
Conscious of the sound
Of continual music-notes that pour
Softly on our ground
Spreading a veil on memory.

The light illumined everything
With deep quietude
And awakened in our hearts something
More than the rude
Dregs of half-drowsed memory.

More than our ordinary dreams came
Inside the closed walls,
And we were consumed by such a flame
That made our walls
Crumble back out of memory.

We were lifted beyond the room
While the room faded;
We were taken out of the womb
Whom the womb had made:
To recognise a further memory.

We felt no more oppression
Under the ceiling.
We knew no more depression.
Had no more feeling.
And the music remained a memory.

Dawn

The lamps contend with dawn
To hold within their beams for one last hour
The pageantry of the streets.
In the juvenile light the birds
Send from the creepers, trees and chimneys
A morning salutation
To a strolling policeman
Whose sole companion is a smouldering pipe.
Two cats slink by
And taxis scurry past few and far between
And several voices echo and vibrate
To the sound of feet
That sound and again repeat
Loud in this deserted street
And the leaves stir
And the sky clears
And accumulated voices hum
Accelerating and ascending
In the day's crescendo.

Beyond the Speed of Light

Beyond the speed of light there's nothing moves
Where distant suns burn stagnant in the sky.
Day after night the universe revolves.
Darkness and light before our eyes swing by.
How often time hangs heavy on our hands
When every minute is a lifetime gone;
It seems as though a mighty barrier stands
Between our deeds and what needs to be done.

In thought too often we are miles away
Performing acts of utmost urgency
When just so often we are forced to stay
Inactive, equal to complacency.
Yet time is no screen-picture overflowing
Another performance, a second showing.

Crumbling
City

London

Crumbling city! Once mirror of the star-lit heaven
And brilliant in your own splendour too. Now
Streetlights are turned down, blinds drawn and neon-signs even
Torn from the cinema front. Everywhere shadow.

In people's eyes look fear, no sleep, and despair.
Children must feed on hunger, read the pavement
While mother labours to quicken dad's massacre
In this mad-house of profit, interest and rent.

This shadow's magnitude is entirely yours.
But not the depth of night, the sense of darkness.
The will to feel belongs to us and ours;
No, not to armed police, business men and bankers.

Out from the back streets, factories, dark men and women –
A furnace charged to white heat threatens the horizon.

The Serpentine

A span of water, placid and pale,
Lies sleeping under the bridge,
Tremulous only when a gale draws swift fingers
In tuneful lines from edge to edge.

A canoe's keen wedge under a sail
Skims easily through the water;
Meanwhile the moon is under pledge not to assail
So the wind, the still water.

Under the stone-bridge lies the water
That nothing will wake but a gale.

The Thames

A large white rat drifted up the river on its back
Past *HMS PRESIDENT*
That gently swayed
But kept her moorings strained
And taut.
Pieces of wood and other refuse strayed
Between the landing stage and the boat's side
Steep and painted,
Going with the tide
Helpless.
The *ALAIN* tug
With five low-laden barges
Smoked its course
Toward Charing Cross
And the river police dashed past.
'Oh, cannot someone drown these trams
Unbridle the power of the bloody water
To let it clear the dust
That with so much disgust
Pursues with tranquil ease its own peculiar way
Through this vast city.'

The Doors of the Tube

Ghostly things these doors are when they open.
Doors which have no watchmen
Doors which have never known a gentle tap
Have never felt the knocks of anger
Never hid a friend or enemy, a lover or the dead.

Ghostly doors! Handless slide impassionate.
Doors which do not invite
Doors which do not make her hesitate
At the entrance of a room
Belonging to friend or enemy, a lover or the dead.

Ghostly things these doors are when they shut.
Doors which no one shuts
Doors which only let men willing to go out
And close upon them entered
Into these carriages smooth moving through modern catacombs.

In the Park

Men take off their hats to mop their old heads
while everybody's walking slowly
along the pavements through the shade.
The chocolate-man has covered up his wares.
The horses are hot and trot wearily in the Row.
The sheep bleat by the Serpentine, new sheared and thin
in bare continuous monotone.
Bobbing, the ducks waddle through the grass to avoid
inebriated steps of a full-fledged Cygnet.
A tattered 'Scrap of Paper'
fixed to the points of the iron rails
is sensitive to air.

Night (1)

Silence can be found
Only where the roads pass through
From thoroughfare to thoroughfare;
Tis true and yet untrue
For women sitting in saloons
Laugh and irritate the air
Appreciating humour over beer.

Here I am again
Among chattering lamps
To Covent Garden bound
Where the few that are found
Speak, walk and look
(described in a book)
And drunk they steer
Down the difficult pavements.

How pale and wearied with forbidden love
The men and women seem!
A van, like a cage drove past the market
Carrying new flowers for the morrow's sale.

Night (2)

I shall endeavour
To lose myself in the lonely streets
(though packed with people and the traffic's stir)
To follow my shadow down dark retreats
Further and further.

I'll strive to leave the world alone
Or else in some cheap cinema
Watch fabulous love's desires fulfilled
And dread what might have been
Or what may come.

I Thought
England Safe

Thaelmann

Barred, the inflexible day – cell walls
stone-flat concrete and bricks, sky out of reach,
and in chains – Thaelmann. The man built,
like the fugitive in the hay stack, the would-be clerk,
a world against oppression, war on each
past year that spreads its avalanche of dark
over the new trees, the beginning, the green success.

Only the light of invincible early morning.
Only the distinct rattle of the world
dragging fetters. Only the prison bell rings.
And keys, voices of men and warders, unlocked doors
shut like an empty plate, and the grey old
evening twilight. Night brings a poverty of stars
window bound. And the whisper of all moving.

The Asturian Miners

Suddenly risen after years of quiet digging
No more like coal they've raised from the dug shaft
No more do they submit
To the pick, the wage-cut, and the easy talk
The hunger that eats away their soft guts.
Not gods. Nor great men. Not heavy headed
Men. Not sons of Thor or Samson who might wield
Weapons of immense size. Nor brutes. These
Are wrought of hunger, are sons of women,
Sons of quarrels shouted down the street
Sons of laughter piercing from a basement
Children of defeat, heroes 'to arms!'
Technicians, workmen, human – that's them.

Their lips pressed white for lack of food
And the black dust hollows out their white eyes
A bitter hatred nursed
In a deep sadness to which only they know
How to respond with life itself fighting.
And at other times with sensitive deeds
With tenderness, fatiguing patience, able
Are the horny knuckles, scarred hands, capable.
Out there beyond the latest crest – over –
Huge thunder clouds ride slowly warning black.
Our work-mates' bodies lie bleeding at the mouth,
And dull red patches saturate their clothes
Recently cleaned by the hands of their girls.

England

I thought England green with pleasant valleys
dividing smooth fields rich to stroke
to lie with one's face sideways in the grass
watching a stretch of trembling water.

From doors of dark and grimy alleys
in huge spreading cities, breathing smoke,
through black cracks in curtained windows
pale houses queer.

I thought England safe where the brook
broke silence over the pebbles, where the rows
of houses parallel to the sky over the hill
where the white clouds, smoke, look
to see what we're doing, asking
'Help the people of Spain.'

From the valleys grey with dust
from the hopeless homes of people
from the alleys long forgotten
by the scum who fight against us
by the rich who starve the people
from ragged clothes and dirty pockets
sewn and cleaned a thousand times
comes the will to pay the price
comes the penny's mighty sacrifice
comes the warmth of friendliness.

England's subdued voices tell
how Freedom strode inside the closed forest of Sherwood.
Breath of England!
How men marched from North and South and East and West on
London.
Heart of England!
How they would mould it all
and name it after them
England.

February 1939

Abyssinia

All foreign powers gather for her blood.

Black Africa, primeval Africa! And Nile –
along whose banks luxurious Egypt went
in search of Rome, of youthful Rome –
here looks a man down on the ugly gnome
of 'black' Italy. Great Caesar, too great! Now
all the hideous opposite of Caesar,
murdered by a nightmare in the Capitol,
stalks the ruins lit by a hollow moon,
a cheap forgery and imitation.

Egypt died long ago, and with her, Rome
lies in the bed of the continuous Nile
pouring out of Africa.

The stream turns?
Will Africa now conquer all her past?

September 1935

Wherever Green Wheat Flows

Wherever green wheat flows over the hills
And earth, combed by the plough, falls
On the world's shoulders. Wherever light fills
Breaks in woods, windows in prison walls.

Wherever people meet and sing together –
You said, 'Go sing, join in the singing too,' –
Where an aeroplane darts by a feather
In space, and a child says something new.

Whenever some old peasant woman sleeps
And workmen have wiped their greasy hands
After a hard day. Or where the radio sweeps
Across the frontier to further lands

Calling all men by one name 'Brother' –
Oh Mother of Life, you'll be their young mother.

The last two lines in Branson's handwritten version of
the poem. This is part of a larger piece.

People Draw Their Curtains Close

People draw their curtains close
To keep the light within
And the night
Without.
The trees appear a silver-grey
Green-tinted
Under the evening's sensitive brush.

Two young men with a mandolin
In the less frequented parts
Sing
Valencia
And only stop when coins drop
Or cease to fall.

The lamps throw out their radiating beams
To take dominion of the shadowed roads.
The wireless utters varied sounds
Into closely lighted rooms.

The Continental Restaurant's empty now.

Today My Eyes

Today my eyes have felt like jets of flame
Burning their way into my head. The strain
Of constant searching through the world to gain
More light on light, the fact behind a name,
The stark reality that prompted fame
To build a dance-hall on the skulls of pain,
Has hurt these instruments. But to remain
Seeing and sightless is a deeper shame.

Blind are the windows of an empty home
Although they stare into the face of heaven.
They too are blind who travel far and roam
The world while they don't know their own street even.
The dead deserve no eyes who from their birth
Neglect to learn the beauty of the earth.

A Handkerchief Waved from a Parting Train

A handkerchief waved from a parting train
A welcome from the window.
A memory lingers after huge events
Unwilling to leave peace
Or minimise striving.
The soft cocoon
That makes life possible
Protecting the slow change
And development of men
From the scorching sun.
A drink of water
To moist the tongue
Of the earth lost among
This desert of burning stars.
Promising rain and new life.
Seed to the bumper crop
Least thought to greatest art.

A gull settled on the sea
A gull soaring up the side of cliffs
Reminds the soldier in distress
Of familiar things he loved back home
Clean cups and his wife in summer dress.
Tells the prisoner in his loneliness
Time shares his solitude and the years
Move round to the hour of freedom.
Cools the traveller's burning feet.
Eases the heated brain. Brings sleep.
Sails beyond the sea into space
Words become music, colours sing
Sounds burst into flame
Raising life from the dead-still earth
Movement springs from the written word
Grain from the furrowed land.
Smiles to entice the love-sick youth

Teasing, fleeting, mistress. Truth
Fools the flights of self-conceit
With airy nothingness complete.
Breaks into monotony. Makes
Inquisitive people staring at a fatal accident.
Unemployed shuffling into the labour exchange.
Patience rising into demonstration, food queue into riot.
An audience waiting for the play to begin.
A mass meeting, listening, some shouting, at a factory gate.
Massed like a mountain range along the edge of the world.
Pompous and easily dispelled by a breath of fresh air.
A sermon on ignorance to confuse the dreamer.
Warning little men of storms equal to the seas they ride
Monstrous waves of silence surge above the earth's side.

A bird disappears in the mist
Shielding the mountain summit.
First whispered talks of treason
Veils the moon's face on a mysterious night.
Hides her shame
As she guides the bomber-plane
On its midnight task
Of sowing death –

But once there were no clouds
Where the moon shone
To light the golden corn
In the Ukraine
Helping the peasants
Gather in the harvest
From the flames of war
And the enemy's hunger.
Makes a daring flight against the sun
Prophesying
Man's challenge to the past, flying.

Evening

Somewhere the stream is broad. Somewhere the Swan
Paddling against the inconvenient flow
Opens a white wing to clean and moves on
Unconscious that the very stream is slow

And wide: unaware that it is so deep
Save in the shallows where the green weeds sway
And there the water grows food. In half sleep
A fish knows nothing of the liquid day

That goes along whereon the white bird glides
Repeating itself inadvertently. Tall
Reeds lean and whisper over the steep sides –
Good shelter for the rat – enveloping all

And the first cool of evening. Here
From the usual shade night spreads everywhere.

Soldier Just Take a Look

Soldier just take a look at that bright moon
Which lights the bomber to some new grave's side.
Gone are the times of romance! Over wide
Acres of night death ploughs the ruts of doom
Changing the destiny of tomb and womb.
Think if you've time that I'm in bed to hide
From steel although aware the battle's tide
Plunges on to overwhelm me so soon.

Night after night when I let up the blind
Soon as the bugles call Turn in! Lights out!
Moonlight breaks through the window and the mind
Hoping for sleep is stormed by thoughts about
You, Red Army men, who now for all mankind
Fight with no rest till Fascism ends in rout.

Prisoner

San Pedro

A foreign darkness fills the air tonight.
The moon betrays this unfamiliar scene.
Strange creatures, shadow-ghosts of what had been
Live with no aim than groping through half-light,
Talk dreamily, walk wandering, delight
In trivial acts that formerly would mean
Nothing. A livid memory, this lean
Ill-clad rabble of a lost dreaded might.

Look longer, deeper, the accustomed eyes
Know more than quick appearances can tell.
These fools, this shoddy crowd, this dirt, are lies
Their idiot captors wantonly compel.
These men are giants chained down from the skies
To congregate an old and empty hell.

The Nightingale

You spent your voice upon the midnight air
Here, when we were newcomers, you were alone.
No one listened. Your music died to share
Each tedious darkness with the deaf-mute moon.

A sleepless captive swears to hear you sing
Whom his sorrow renders still. We too cower
Awake under the dead blanket thinking
Of that illusive freedom you echo each hour.

And even through the shouting of the guard,
Their chain of noise, we hear you secret bird,
Their strength, their arrogance, though bayonet proud,
Can't still the voice humanity has heard.

Your silence is articulate when you
Must be obedient, sing when ordered to.

San Pedro, 1938

To the German Anti-Fascists in San Pedro

The evening went beyond the bars, passed by us
His face at the window
His voice in a frame
He 'who ought to be shot' and will be
when the Nazis get him home.
He was singing
this German prisoner, self-exiled workman,
common songs of the beer-garden in his home town.
Singing to memories of friends
who could not hear.
And others, some half dozen, sang too.

I have lain in my blanket at night
kept awake by lice and a dry itching skin
looked at the blue window panes broken
with a star up in one corner.
Outside a night-bird intensely sings
unseen and to no-one.
Only to memories of friends did he sing?
Only to the deaf ears of these ghosts?
Was there meaning in his song, or meaningless
Like that of the nightingale?
Mere repetition of a few notes through centuries
with no gain
Just a song of the beer-garden?

In the strains of music
In the discipline of song
This prisoner, the captive voice
sang of the freedom in trees, of cloud and wind
the movement of men on bicycles, hiking,
of animals not afraid of leaving their cages
who do not need the safety of their cell
the security of a gaol.

He sang the promise of a dream
sometime come true, of free men
whose homes are not prisons,
beds not graves, play not in murder,
work for creation.

This German sang to us of home
Our heritage in one another
Comrade, Brother – no foreigner.

San Pedro, 1938

On the Statue of Christ, Palencia (1)

Still symmetry! Is this our human aim?
Knowing conceit! Should child of woman born
live perfect death to reach a deathless fame?
Her child still-born! Spain's body mangled, torn.

Historic judgement no confusion mars.
Perhaps this statue climbs upon the hill
better to win the plenitude of stars:
Ride with the sun beyond earth's window sill.

Perhaps it cheats the sight its splendour bars,
Its high pretence to life lives on to kill.

On the Statue of Christ, Palencia (2)

When I first saw this venerable stone
Statue standing up against the sunrise
I learnt how vast it was to be alone
To pause in solitude before men's eyes,

Not to move while the day's wide motion threw
The sun above all else, whose blazing heat
Parched tongues to flame, white-powdered roads; and drew
the cool of evening past the statue's feet.

At night dogs howl, the firmament spins round,
Dark is the noise of unseen insects' wings,
And yet I know you are on your high mound
Straight, upright, fixed, immune to living things.

Dead as a rock memento of the past
Life's immortality in death held fast.

Palencia, 1938

By the Canal Castilla

It is difficult to think
of the noise of guns while men die
while we sit and in the hot sun lie
beside the lazy still water of the canal.

Get up, dive and shatter illusion!

The guard's bayonet splinters the sun.
A gilded iris shrivels up.
A poppy's crimson cup
breaks petal by petal to the wind.
That carries memories
of other trees, stretches of water, wings.

An unseen shadow sings.
Everything waits what the next journey brings –
Even the authorities.

Sunset

Like a new cut on a young girl's shoulder
the sun left a crimson scar.
Through barbed wire
we can feel the day's passing
and evening
warns us of night, the complete end.

Palencia, 1938

A Sunday Afternoon

A delicate breeze sufficient to stir
Light dust, a little leaf, by an insect's wing

Dance music on the wireless; between prisoner
And a girl dressed like a rose, a smile.

A leaf, a frog, a shadow, a piece of paper
A trickle of water, reading, writing
These things on a stillness deeper than all
Took a whole afternoon to drift with the canal.

Palencia, 1938

The Prisoner's Outlook

Sun swayed, huge flower, from morning to night
Our neck hurt watching the pendulous flight.
The chords of the heart were strained to repeat
Wide beat, beat, throb of the day-great pulse beat.
As we lay in the grass looking up sky wide
Dangled the senseless sword from side to side.
The moon's recurrence, stars persistence,
Speed kills, but speed so vast is slow suspense,
Torments the quicker springs, wearies the brain,
Stretches quick light back to its end again
After eternity of search and travel
Millions of times died in an eye's pupil
Mutinous water, tides, tropic rain, attend
Monotonous as clouds and wind with no end.
A long white road bending back against itself –
War not to end wars. Sentence for life
No chance to repeat, no hope for reprieve.

Palencia, 1938

In the Camp

The storm has cleared the air
but not barbed wire.
Here we can bask in the sun,
should our eyes have forgotten,
pointed at by the guard's bayonet.

We're like young trees set
on a wide landscape and mountain
in a picture for ever certain.
Clouds pass and fine weather
and with them the liberty we long for.

Palencia, 1938

Death Sentence Commuted to Thirty Years

When this sunrise put the question, 'why
should birds sing?' Even the machine-gun
kills in rhythm. For the ordinary eye
enjoys the redness in blood, the purple of wine,
Death's proud carnation
a murdered man twists at the corner of his mouth.

While we sat down by the river, barbed wire
was stretched between us and a circling cloud
to emphasise our horizon, perpetual window,
wall's edge, the beat of a guard on duty.
Caged in, to see a star, to think the world,
to live life's compass in a flat gravel yard,

The homeward rail imagination ran
outdistanced time with modern mockery.
Slow passed each day, compiled a week,
our patient waiting streamed by the prison bars
till we grew tired of counting; only knew
Death is no sudden, but reiterated speed.

On Dreaming of Home

Silver wings travel like sunlight across the field.
The wind creates waves over long grass and sea.
Snow and cloud crest mountains. Still eternity!

Not even sunlight can rise like the aeroplanes
Surge over the edge of the moon, oceans and field,
Ride the motion of time, thinking, thought free
Waves of the fixed mind, span distances, outstrip
The evening star, the course of the lagging moon,
And the recurrent sun, completed the millionth lap.

Yes, we can take off, easily leave and circle
Into the course of our desires. But where?
Where to land? Where is the lettering of your name,
That spells the safe hangar, aerodrome and home?

No good the map of the will alone, not enough
The sure imagination, swiftest dream,
Most certain and accurate chart of the mind's eye.
These are most necessary, but waiting between
Are storm clouds no sane pilot dares to enter,
Are moods of weather and daylight shutting in,
And white mists, the shrouds of certain death,
And the variable wind, uncertain friend.

More, there is the gap from mind to mind
Which has not yet revealed its winged machine;
No-one has crossed. Though thought has left its hangar
Risen with ease and powerful at the start,
Soared over barbed wire, walls, made the near world
Seem distant or forgotten; soon has followed
A quick return or inevitable crash.

Daring friends are keen with good advice:
'Don't dream, don't let the brain tick over, don't
Pour fuel into the engine of the mind, don't
Test the ailerons, or think of one direction.
Stay in the club-house and have another drink.'

But we are pioneers, we who dream and think.
Dream of wide spaces that sever man from man.
Think out the journey and in detailed plan
Of the end. Even though we crash soon and near,
Our thought's beginning is our dream's conqueror.

Palencia, 1938

We Are The People...

The General Didn't Know

The general didn't know there was so much mud
that men sank in it, were choked with it, and died
carrying out his orders which had to be obeyed
on penalty of death. That's why his plan miscarried.
He told us this, with drinks and laughter,
long after the war was over.
He taught us then to understand.
We are the soldiers. We are the bombed.
We are the routed, the wounded, the dead.

No matter our name – what the papers call us:
British or Russian, French or Nazis.

We are the people those bombs hit again –
and again – there's always printer's ink
for tomorrow's press – and again –
there's always plenty of drink
for the General Staff – and again
until we realise WE are the men, the women,
the children killed in the press
by the generals for the rich
who have no feelings, cannot feel our pain.

Blackout

New stars on wing-tips with engines
can cut through the night we sleep in.

Dazzle this sleep with a neon-sign
but don't let the starlight in.

Switch on the street lights at once
the night shift's due to begin.

We can't stop the gangsters' machine-gun
through the blackout that's shut us in.

April 1939

May First

Over the peoples of Europe dying and dead
the barbed wire of the concentration camp has spread
to new territories – Spain, now France –
and will take England too unless *we* advance
like the Workers' and Peasants' Army that came in the nick of time
to rescue half Poland, to hurl Baron Mannheim
back from the gates of Leningrad. We can.
There's no difference between us and Russians, man for man,
but this: they march on where we hold back through doubt.
They slung their rich men and their traitors out
while we continue as we are, let down, delayed,
confused, fooled, double-crossed and finally betrayed
by those who rule us throned on our little finger.

Not always has it been like this in England. Here
for centuries the peasants took their stand
fighting that those who worked should own the land
not Baron, Priest or King. They failed –
though never for want of knowing the power they held.
Whereas our fathers lived and laboured, scattered over the country.
We are organised in mine, workshop and factory,
and huge town. Think of the difficulty the peasant had
to collect an army. *We* as quick as the word,
can turn out in millions, possess the streets,
bring industry to a standstill, are disciplined; such feats
even the Chartists could not emulate, yet they
were never slow in rising to make the rich pay
for all their degradation. That movement died,
with victory following after, but it supplied
with France and Germany the component parts
to make up modern communism. That spectre which haunts
today the whole world.

Have you forgotten
How Karl Marx and Frederick Engels lived in London,
worked in London, led from London the Paris Commune,
American Labour, Germans against Bismarck. How Lenin
here, in our London, raised high the torch of progress,
printed *Iskra*, the spark that glowed in the darkness
of Imperialism and Tsardom, and from the debris of war
burst into the splendour of the USSR.

There's no corner of the world today where men work
in factory or field but in bated breath they speak
of Freedom. Soldiers want peace. Peace and Freedom
and Bread. And someone explains 'that's Communism'.
The wireless warns against Communism. The gutter press
screams against Communism. The Labour Leaders
shriek against Communism. All the time mankind
longs for Freedom, Peace and Bread. That's why we must find
the path to their understanding, the same path
shown to us in the Manifesto, the birth-
certificate of the new man, the free man.

Shame!
That when a Spaniard lay dying he cursed the name
of Britain. Pity the little children
who die so horribly, so young, for Britain
in Barcelona, India, Norway, Finland, China –
What use is our city when Britain is the murderer?
Pity and Charity are the hand-rags of Slavery.

Though the Irish curse, though the Spaniard die angrily
hating us, they are wrong. Our men and women
are the same that Tom Mann led. The same as when
our dockers stopped the Jolly George. The same as those
who in nine short days in nineteen-twenty-six rose
almost to power. The same who marched on May First
challenging with Red Banners (our flags) the cursed
Union Jack and pomp of coronation. Bone of their bone
with the five hundred men of the British Battalion
who died in Spain.

Today is MAY FIRST

                                    We take this oath,
No matter the consequence to ourselves – life or death –
we pledge our whole strength to raise once again
the banner of liberty, the banner of Englishmen.
Though the Red Flag may now be down under,
in our hands we'll lift it to flutter and thunder
in the storm of our movement, to head the assault
against the world's tyrants who rule through our fault.
Wars make the rich richer, and the poor poorer
except when the poor fight the rich to be master.
The call is 'to arm'; we trumpet that call
to toiling humanity. End once and for all
the exploitation of man by man and rich men's wars.
Let every Englishman fight for this cause –
Communism is English! Freedom is ours!

May 1940

The Soviet People Speak

Revenge vengeance since against us risen
Refused to meet our request to resist.
Stupid prejudice asserted a twist
In news, in information, in reason.
Insane ignorance this. This condition
Allowed the swelled lazy rich to enlist
Their destructive service just to assist
In treason, intrigue, selling your nation.

These we shot years past knowing the danger
Already there where we easily saw
Expand, would explode, between friend-stranger,
Hero-devil, today devil before
Leader, saviour. Now our long-tried anger
Released from restraint insists once more – war!

Perham Down 1941

Reveille

Death is vanishing.

Challenge with song
Of beautiful spring
This winter long
We're passing.

Wake up young soldier!
How much longer
Will you listen
To the tread of battalions
The roll of divisions
Ringing in your ears from the street below,
In the bulletins
from Moscow?

Get up young soldier!

March on to the thunder of tanks.
Rise up with the aeroplane.
Cry out to the Red Army, 'Thanks
We can strike again.'

You're young
You're strong

Stand up!

Life is beginning.

Perham Down, 1941

To Rupert Brooke

What good is it that you should understand
And feel the beauty of our English tongue
When from life's orchestra you've only wrung
Some trivial notes, an echo of the grand
Tradition of poets that belong to England
And ended when the sightless Milton flung
His vision against night, when Shelley sung
To lend humanity a poet's hand.

They did not mean to take the place of strife
Who wrote the dreams and actions of mankind,
They fought in their own way. They knew the need
To stop the will of man from going blind,
They led the sick from suicide to life,
They strained their art to mingle word and deed.

Perham Down 1941

Bombed Again

THREE NAZI BASES BOMBED AGAIN

No torture. No pain.
No spine stiff with fear.
Just a poster
A reminder
that the Airforce is a decisive factor.

I spoke to a bus conductor,
an old soldier
about Norway – the bloody massacre there –
who said coldly,
The first lot's bound to be wiped out.

And a man back from Spain
from the war, the wounds, and prison
made a long speech about it
without feeling, without emotion; exactly
like a tram running along lines;
exactly
like girls who go to the factory of a morning
as day must follow night
leaving yesterday forgotten, not caring.

Who bothers to read yesterday's paper again?

The manager put off a hundred men
without thinking of the kids, the women.

Only the man who knows of his mate
no machine but someone to hate,
to love, to laugh with, to fight, not
a hand, a number, a flag, to exploit
to register, to stick on a plan
according to schedule no matter the hurt,
the agony, the MAN.

Where Does
Death Begin?

Thoughts of You

When the edge of day's flag is tattered
Long before hours terminate day's end
In bitter wind,
And birds' wings lag,
And smoke crawls softly from the power-station chimney.

When at the end of a long day's labour
Night scrapes the clodded blade of day
Metallic clean, and engines tire,
Before this fire sleeps,
Thoughts of you drift from the still smouldering embers.

3 July 1942, Gulunche, near Poona

Bombay

Come with me and I will show you,
Almost hidden in the shadow
Of an Indian night,
Pavements strewn with human bodies
That with all the other shit
The authorities forget
Even to worry about.

Here's one
Still lives, though all his flesh has gone.
The vulture remains invisible
Till the meal is insensible,
But Life is not so patient as the vulture,
In India, not so poetical.

Ahmednagar, April 1943

Ships

I have leaned on the quayside of this world
And seen life glide inevitably away
On the ocean whose only horizon is
Unseen uncertain shore.

I've watched a galleon far to the edge of the West
Wait on the sea till the sun was lowered
Into the hold, and the rising darkness
Fills the sails for the East.

I have found deep in the sands of time
The skeleton of some long-buried ship
That in its prime split waves and like an arrow
Pierced storms to gain a fiord.

I have played with fragile sailing boats
Running round the pond's edge. Stood helpless by
Shipwrecks in miniature. And know the joy
Of reaching the far side.

I have been carried many weeks of miles
Well packed like merchandise for abroad
When only the thin shell of destiny buoyed
Soldiers to come back alive.

I have looked at crafts made by simple fishermen,
Built as they built them a thousand years past –
Long has that tiny village stood still
Karwar, against the tides.

I have walked aboard a liner so vast,
It felt as though I stood again on land,
Which barely swayed against the towering blast
Of huge collapsing waves.

From deck rails I have read the endless water,
As though my finger moved across a map
I searched in the wide expanse at my feet
The harbour I longed for.

But still I have one ship to travel by
It sails no seas yet brings an exile home
It goes no place yet needs a pilot. I
Would steer my people free.

Free from the chains that weigh the bows down,
Loose from the refuse that drags a blunted keel.
Clear decks for action! With steam and sail
Escape the dockside grasp.

Then we shall climb among the cliffs and breathe
Fresh winds fanned by the passing stars
And chart new courses for the ships we've dreamed
To ride the sky-deep seas.

Ahmednagar, April 1943

I Can Hear the Sea-Waves

I can hear the sea-waves breaking on the shore
       I can hear the buses passing down the street,
I think the human voices ask 'How long before,
       How many waves and buses pass before we meet?'

My candle burns the wick of time low down,
       While in night-silence, history turns the pages.
Wars and religion, imperial Gods are gone.
       The pavement where they trod winds through the
ages.

My doors are shut. Yet in the world outside
Humanity in birth-pangs gets no sleep.
The sea prepares to swell a further tide,
       Life hesitates before the final leap.

To end all strife by elemental force.
       Even the slightest touch will leave its mark.
In endless stream the traffic flows its course,
       And bit by bit recedes into the dark.

On Guard

Sleep on, sentries, through your turn of duty,
The night is dark, stressed by the bugle moon
These insects warn you of the futility
Of mistaking lights and flying out of turn.

Look how they beat against the glass!
With frenzied repetition they are stunned.
Yet had they made no flight to reach false stars
Death would have been a sleep with no wings singed.

Sleep on, sentries, while your beds are safe.
Your sanity commends you to long nights.
These brainless idiots emulate the brave
Who, in their madness, dare celestial flights.

Without a hope of getting back alive.
Sleep on, you sentries, no need to wake up now.
Who was the fool is walking on your grave;
He met the new day rising while you slept, long ago.

Gulunche, India, 3 October 1942

Men Condemned

... Men condemned for years on end
To suffer freedom to do nothing.
The white-washed sky is their cell walls
And earth the floor they walk along
To nowhere. Everything is theirs
Trees, fields, birds, wealth, tanks, gems,
So long as they don't do, don't think, don't
Want to buy with their wages,
Build with their hands and enjoy
Life that is living. They've been warned
'Who wants to take the storm up in both hands
And break this calm to smithereens
Shall go to prison.' This dungeon echoes
The song of birds, people's voices
With the depths of fruitless nothingness,
Emptiness, limitless space,
Where to do nothing by compulsion –
'a wolf clothed in a lamb's white skin' –
Is Freedom which compels men to do nothing.

Ahmednagar, July 1943

When I Come Back

When I come back after this long journey
(Some have claimed to return from the dead,
Hence the great temples built beside slums)
And I meet you, stranger, on the platform.
Your face I dimly remember among many,
I look for the signs I want, little gestures –
Your tiny hand, so friendly touching,
And the firm but gentle leading of your arm towards home.

Yes, it's you alright, but even so
The long time we've been away makes me shy.
(So deeply susceptible is humanity
To the need for trust in someone other)
Shy because I wouldn't tread too hard
On the rare mosaic of our comradeship
From the days when we knew each other well.
And timid because like time we haven't stood still.

Then we will talk of all kinds of things.
But neither will take note of the words nor meaning
Only listen for the loved music of the voice
That is familiar even after so much silence.
You will prompt me to speak and I as well
With quiet applause will ask you to say again
Anything you like to prevent the return
Even a little longer of our separation.

When I am sure that you are you and no dream.
How often my longing was peopled with hollow ghosts!
And you feel confident that we are really met.
Then will we want to test our assurances;
Feel the warmth of our breathing, the softness
Of your breasts along with the movement,
Caressing and fervent holding of body
To body. To close our eyes and sleep completely.

After more words will gather meaning as we speak
Each will have much to tell of what happened
Changes in outlook, new circumstances
The foundations on which with act upon thought
We build a new life. Put into practice
The schemes we visualised on a grey London evening
And under an Indian sun meet and change and merge –
And we'll climb up the steps where hovels once levelled
the world.

Orders for Landing

Today we got our orders for tomorrow,
A few brief sentences as a title page
Preludes a book. Each one wonders how
The story will turn out. What's over the edge?

Yesterday, far as memory spreads back
The shifting incidents of daily life,
Lies at our feet, where we stand upon the deck
Always moving somewhere – self away from self.

It is I who move. I who will look again
To find the I that searched and could not see
Exactly the I that am. Had I but taken
I as the recurrent particle of continuous We!

There's no unknown to him who reads the sea,
For whom the horizon predicts the certain land.
Like words we live, self-lost in history.
We sink like waves into the endless end.

5 December 1943

Jagged Rocks

Jagged rocks jutting out towards the sea
An ox skull white on the bleached sun-dry earth
Dead wood once a forest giant-tree
Rotted, worm tunnelled, nothing worth –
All these time scatters along his path
Round boulders smoothed by a stream
dead... Like a peasant's bowl,
A man's head buried in his place of birth
Millions of years old.

25 December 1943

Millions of Years Old

Millions of years old – over the whole
Hangs the universe like a dome
Pillared on mountains, that fade into their own height,
Breaking through dense jungle-shade to white,
And higher yet into the burning night,
Star-spluttering and belching darkness.
Over the whole spread a silent vastness
So still, the silence recoiled on itself
And broke to pieces in a myriad whispers –
A mountain stream worming its way to the sea –
The hushed shifting of sand before the breakers,
Heard from miles beyond the forest's edge –
Insects' wings brushing the breathless air –
A leaf falling on leaves and the drip of dew,
Then through the night the howl of homeless dogs
To hurl the stillness back into no noise.
When from the hills, not seen till touching the trees,
Morning, like a flock of flamingoes, wings
To settle in the branches and spread across the fields.

Burma, 4 January 1944

Without Time

I lay on my back on the deck looking up
At a star which swayed from side to side
In a sea of perpetual space.
Time was a secret to everything living
For fear that the dead might learn,
There lying among sea-weed and broken ships
Fish – haunted and watched
They'd been swindled
And take revenge
Turn all so that the star I see
Is a grain of sand in the depth of eternity
Or an eye looking at me.

Where Light Breaks Up

Where light breaks up obscurity for sunrise,
And peace accumulates the parts of storm.
Where death's the sequence of the pregnant womb
An embryo contains the adult's size.
Where mountain peaks hold up the moving skies
Their might is tunnelled by the invidious worm;
Where clouds pile up their cumbersome white form
The flat laborious plain of wheat-fields lies.

Women and children build up the only road
Where overhead the shells of death whine past
And cattle graze indifferent to the din.
I felt perhaps I'd understood at last
By close observance of all that nature showed
'When life has gone, then where does death begin?'

the Burma front, February 1944

Acknowledgements

The help and support of both Rosa Branson and the Marx Memorial Library are gratefully acknowledged.

Some of the poems in the anthology have appeared elsewhere, notably Clive Branson, *British Soldier in India* (Communist Party, 1944), *Cambridge Left, Poetry and the People,* Jim Jump (ed) *Poems from Spain* (Lawrence & Wishart, 2006), Jon Clark, Margot Heinemann *et al* (eds) *Culture and Crisis in Britain in the Thirties* (Lawrence & Wishart, 1979) and Valentine Cunningham (ed) *The Penguin Book of Spanish Civil War Verse* (Penguin 1980).

Notes

A Song: Lenin to Gorky
In the early 1930s Maxim Gorky was regarded as Russia's greatest living novelist. A Marxist, he was, at various times, close to both Lenin and Stalin, but lived in exile until Stalin invited him back to Russia in 1932. He died four years later.

To C Day Lewis
The poet C Day Lewis was a member of the Communist Party in the mid-Thirties but became increasingly disillusioned and left the party in 1938.

Thaelmann
Ernst Thaelmann was the leader of the German Communist Party. Arrested by the Gestapo in 1933, he was shot, on Hitler's personal orders, in 1944.

The Asturian Miners
Asturias is in north-west Spain. In October 1934 the region's coal miners staged an armed revolt which was brutally put down by troops under the direction of the future Fascist dictator Francisco Franco.

Abyssinia
Abyssinia – now Ethiopia – was invaded by Italian troops in October 1935. In Branson's typed version of the poem, the date 25/11/34 is added in pencil.

On the Statue of Christ, Palencia (1)
In the summer of 1938 Branson was moved from San Pedro to a prison camp in Palencia, 55 miles south west of Burgos. Italian-run, it provided a less brutal regime than San Pedro.

May First
1 May 1940 was in the final days of the 'Phoney War'. On 10 May that year German troops began a powerful offensive and by the end of the month, the remnants of the British army had escaped from the beaches at Dunkirk. Three weeks later France surrendered.

The Soviet People Speak
By 1941 Clive Branson was serving with the Royal Armoured Corps, based at Perham Down near Salisbury Plain. His painting and poetry helped him cope with the dead hand of army life. His notebook written at the time includes a string of poems, as well as a scribbled note of train times and places – plans for escaping the monotony of the camp...

Thoughts of You
'While on guard tonight I was thinking of Battersea and wrote this poem...' (in a letter to his wife).